# ARE THE SOUTHERN PRIVATEERSMEN PIRATES?

---

# LETTER

TO THE

## HON. IRA HARRIS,

UNITED STATES SENATOR.

BY CHARLES P. DALY, L.L.D.

FIRST JUDGE OF THE COURT OF COMMON PLEAS OF THE CITY OF NEW YORK.

---

New York:
JAMES B. KIRKER,
599 BROADWAY.
1862.

# ARE SOUTHERN PRIVATEERSMEN PIRATES?

NEW YORK, Dec. 21, 1861.

DEAR SIR,

In compliance with your request at our conversation in Washington, I will put in writing the reasons why the Southern privateersmen should be regarded as prisoners of war, and not as pirates.

Privateering is a lawful mode of warfare, except among those nations who, by treaty, stipulate that they will not, as between themselves, resort to it. Pirates are the general enemies of all mankind—*hostes humani generis;* but privateersmen act under and are subject to the authority of the nation or power by whom they are commissioned. They enter into certain securities that they will respect the rights of neutrals; their vessel is liable to seizure and condemnation if they act illegally, and they wage war only against the Power with which the authority that commissioned them is at war. A privateer does no more than is done by a man-of-war, namely, seize the vessel of the enemy, the prize or booty being distributed as a reward among the captors. The only difference between them is, that the vessel of war is the property of the Government, manned and maintained by it, whilst the other is a private enterprise, undertaken for the same general purpose, and giving guarantees that it will be conducted according to the established usages of war. In short, one is a public, the other a private vessel-of-war, neither of which acquire any right to a prize taken, until the lawfulness of the capture is declared by a competent Court, under whose direction the thing taken is condemned and sold, and the proceeds distributed in such proportion as the law considers equitable. The Government of the United States declined to become a party to the international treaty of Paris, in 1856; and therefore the whole people of the United States—as well those who are now maintaining the Government as those who are in rebellion against it—have never agreed to dispense with privateering, It is not our interest to do so. We are a maritime people, with a large extent of sea-coast, which, whilst it leaves us greatly exposed to attacks by sea, at the same time affords facilities that render privateering, to us, one of our most effective arms in warfare. This was the case in our contest with England in 1812; and should a war now grow out of the affair of the *Trent*, privateering would be indispensable, to enable us to cope with so formidable a Power as that of Great Britain.

A great deal has been written against this mode of warfare, but nations, like individuals, act upon the instinct of self-preservation, and avail themselves of the natural defences which grow out of their situation; and a system, therefore, which enables us to keep but a small navy in peace and improvise a large one in war, will never be relinquished, because nations who have everything to lose, or little to gain, by its continuance, desire that it should be generally abolished.

Being then a legitimate mode of making war, what is the difference between the Southern soldier who takes up arms against the Government of the United States on the land, and the Southern privateersman who does the same upon the water? Practically there is none, and if one should be held and exchanged as a prisoner of war, the other is equally entitled to the privilege. The Court before which the crew of the *Jefferson Davis* were convicted as pirates, held that they could not be regarded as privateers, upon the ground that they were not acting under the authority of an independent State, with the recognized rights of sovereignty. This objection applies equally to the man-of-warsmen in the Southern fleets, and to every soldier in the Southern army, none of whom are acting under the authority of a recognized Government. The Constitution defines treason to be the levying of war against the United States, and the giving of aid and comfort to its enemies. All of them are engaged in doing this. The guilt of the one is precisely the same as that of the other. There is not and cannot be, in this respect, any difference between them. Why then is the mariner distinguished from the soldier, as pursuing the infamous calling of a pirate? If, as the Courts have held, he cannot be considered as a privateersman from the want of the authority of a recognised Government, does it necessarily follow that he is or must be a pirate? The pirate is the Ishmaelite of the ocean, submitting to no law and recognizing no authority human or divine. An outlaw setting all the restraints of society at defiance, whose object unrelieved by any other motive, is plunder, and who in the attainment of that object hesitates at no extent of wickedness. Is this the position of the Southern privateersman? It was shown in the case of the *Jefferson Davis*, that all the formalities which governments require in the fitting out of privateers had been scrupulously complied with, a fact which indicates that the Southern privateersman holds a very different position from that of the marine freebooter, inasmuch as he is acting under the authority and is subject to the control of what he at least regards as a government. His true position is that of a rebel upon the ocean. As a mariner it is the sphere of his activity, and its pursuits are those on which he depends for a livelihood; and though it be conceded that he is attracted to the kind of service upon which he enters by the hope of large pecuniary profits, is he not as well as the soldier entitled to the consideration that he may also be influenced by a mixed motive? It is the motive that settles whether an act is criminal or not. It is by that test that we determine, in the taking of property by force, whether the act was a robbery or a trespass. Judging the Southern mariner then by this standard, can we say that he is not swayed by the same passions, influenced by the same excitement, and imbued with the same political opinions, that have led such a multitude of men to take part in this rebellion? And if he is, does not that distinguish him from the common criminal?

The act which he has committed—that of rising in arms to overthrow the Government, and to sever one part of its territory from the rest,—is more injurious to the nation than any damage that can be inflicted by the predatory acts of the pirate. It is the gravest and weightiest offence that a citizen can commit; but mankind have always distinguished between political offences and meaner and more mercenary crimes, a distinction which Coke, the profoundest of English jurists, had in view when he says that "those things which are of the highest criminality may be of the least disgrace." Of this political offence the Southern privateersman is guilty, but he is not a pirate, and the inconsistency of attempting to treat him as such is forcibly illustrated by a case in point from our own annals. On the breaking out of the American revolution a number of privateers were equipped by the colonists, first under the sanction of the State of Massachusetts and afterwards by the authority of Congress; and on the 28th of February, 1777, an act was passed by the British parliament, under the provisions of which any colonist, taking part in privateering, was declared to be a pirate; and if taken he was to be committed by any magistrate to the common jail upon the charge of piracy, and there detained until the king or privy council should determine whether it was expedient or not to try him for that offence. This act, which was framed by Lord Thurlow, a man of an unscrupulous, arbitrary and despotic character, was strenuously opposed upon its passage by Fox, Dunning, Barre, and all the liberal members of parliament, and was denounced by Burke in the severest terms in his celebrated letter to the sheriffs of Bristol: "The persons," he said, "who make a naval war upon us in consequence of the present troubles, may be rebels; but to call or treat them as pirates, is to confound the natural distinction of things, and the nature of crimes. * * The general sense of mankind tells me that those offences which may possibly arise from mistaken virtue, are not in the class of infamous actions," and he further remarked that if Lord Balmanno, in the Scotch rebellion, had driven off the cattle of twenty clans, he would have thought it a low juggle, unworthy of the English judicature, to have tried him for felony as a stealer of cows. The act was successively renewed every year until near the close of the war; and during that period some 230 persons were detained under it in the English jails. But as a preventive measure it accomplished nothing. Privateering continued unabated, and at last the persons so confined were exchanged under an act introduced through the influence of General Burgoyne.

As all who have participated in the rebellion are alike guilty of the same political offence, and as there is in point of fact no difference between them, the question then arises—is every seaman or soldier taken in arms against the Government to be hung as a traitor or pirate?

If the matter is to be left to the Courts, conviction and the sentence of death must follow in every instance. In the case of the *Jefferson Davis*, the Court said, that during civil war, in which hostilities are prosecuted on an extended scale, persons in arms against the established Government, captured by its naval and military forces, are often treated not as traitors or pirates, but according to the humane usages of war. They are detained as prisoners until exchanged or discharged on parole, or if surrendered to the civil authorities and convicted, they are respited or pardoned; but the Court said that this was a matter with which courts and juries had nothing to do. That it was purely a question of governmental policy, depending upon the decision of the executive or legislative departments of the Government, and not upon its judicial organs.

If this view be correct, the disposition of this matter rests exclusively with the Government, and its decision must be pronounced sooner or later, as every day increases the complication and difficulty growing out of the present state of things. Are the Courts to go on? Is the Government prepared to say that every man in arms against the United States, upon the land or upon the water, is to be tried and executed as a traitor or pirate?—either upon the ground that it is right, or upon the supposition that it will prove an effective means of suppressing this rebellion? That policy was tried by the Duke of Alva, in the revolt of the seven provinces of the Netherlands, and 18,000 persons, by his orders, suffered death upon the scaffold; the result being a more desperate resistance, the sympathy of surrounding nations, and the ultimate independence of the Dutch.

Neither the Constitution of the United States, nor the

act against piracy, were framed in view of any such state of things as that which now exists. The civil war now prevailing is, in its magnitude, beyond anything previously known in history. The revolting States hold possession of a large portion of the territory of the Union, embracing a great extent of sea-coast and including some of our principal cities and harbors. They hold forcible possession of it by means of an army estimated at 400,000 men, and are practically exercising over it all the power and authority of Government. They claim to have separated from the United States, to have founded a Government of their own, and are in armed resistance to maintain it. To reduce them to obedience and to recover that of which they hold forcible possession, it has been necessary for us to resort to military means of more than corresponding magnitude, until the combatants on both sides have reached to the prodigious number of a million of men. The principal nations of Europe recognizing this state of things, have conceded to the rebellious States the rights of belligerents, a course of which we have no reason to complain, as we did precisely the same thing toward the States of South America in their revolt against the Government of Spain. It is natural that we should have hesitated to consider the Southern States in the light of belligerents before the rebellion had expanded to its present proportions; but now we cannot, if we would, shut our eyes to the fact, that war, and war upon a more extensive scale than usually takes place between contending nations, actually exists. It is now, and it will continue to be, carried on upon both sides, by a resort to all the means and appliances known to modern warfare; and unless we are to fall back into the barbarism of the middle ages, we must observe in its conduct those humane usages in the treatment and exchange of prisoners, which modern civilization has shown to be equally the dictates of humanity and of policy.

For every seaman that we have arrested as a pirate, they have incarcerated a Northern soldier, to be dealt with exactly as we do by the privateersman. We have convicted as pirates four of the crew of the *Jefferson Davis*, and there are others in New York awaiting trial. Are these men to be executed? If they are, then by that act we deliberately consign to death a number of our own officers and soldiers, most of whom owe their captivity and present peril to the heroic courage with which they stood by their colors on a day of disastrous flight and panic.

If such a course is to be pursued, it will not be very encouraging for the soldier now in arms for the maintenance of the Union, to know that what may be asked of him is to fight upon one side, with the chance of being hanged upon the other; and in face of the enemy, with his line broken, instead of rallying again, he may, in view of the possibility of a halter, consider it prudent to retire before the double danger.

If, on the other hand, we convict these men as criminals and pause there, then the crime of which we have declared them to be guilty is not followed by its necessary consequence, the proper punishment. There is no terror inspired and no check interposed by such a procedure; for the plainest man in the South knows that the motive which restrains us from going further is the fact, that the execution of these men as pirates seals the doom of a corresponding number of our own people—that the account is exactly balanced—that, with ample means of retaliation, they have the power to prevent; or, if mutual blood is to be shed in this way, *we* and not they will have commenced it. By such a course nothing is effected, except to keep our own officers and soldiers in the cells of Southern prisons, subject to that mental torture produced by the uncertainty of their fate, which, with the majority of men, is more difficult to bear than the certainty of death itself,—and oblige them to endure, in the ill-provided and badly conducted prisons in which they are confined, sufferings, the sickening details of which are constantly before us in their published letters to their friends.

"I little thought," writes the gallant Col. Cogswell, of the regular service, "when I faced the storm of bullets at Edwards' Ferry, and escapêd a soldier's death upon the field, that it was only to be left by my country to die upon the gallows." And the nature of their sufferings will be understood when it is told that the noble-hearted and self-sacrificing Col. Corcoran was handcuffed and placed in a solitary cell, with a chain attached to the floor, until the mental excitement produced by this ignominious treatment, combining with a susceptible constitution and the infectious nature of the locality, brought on an attack of typhoid fever. Shall this state of things continue? Let us take counsel of our common sense. These men are treated as criminals, because, while we give to the Southern soldier the rights of war (for numerous exchanges of soldiers have taken place), we convict the Southern mariner of a crime punishable with death. Is there any reason, even upon the grounds of policy, for making this distinction? We have, by the blockade of the whole Southern coast, cut the privateersman off from bringing his prize into the ports of the South for adjudication; and the ports of all neutral nations being closed against him for such a purpose, he is deprived of the means of making lawful prizes, and must eventually convert his vessel into a ship-of-war, or degenerate into a pirate, by unlawful acts which will make him amenable to the tribunal of every civilized nation. The comparative injury that may be done to our commerce by the few privateers which it will now be in the power of the rebellious States to maintain upon the ocean, is as nothing compared to the disastrous and lasting consequences to the whole nation, to its industry, its commerce and its future, that would grow out of making this war one of retaliatory vengeance. We have the fruitful experience of history to admonish us that in such acts are sown the seeds of the dissolution of nations and especially of republics. By according to the rebellious States the rights of belligerents, at least to the extent of exchanging prisoners, whether privateersmen, man-of-war's me, nor soldiers,—we do not concede to them the rights of sovereignty. There is a well-defined distinction between the two, recognized by the United States Court in the case of Rose *vs.* Himmley, 4 Cranch, 241. One may exist without the other; and by exchanging prisoners, therefore, we concede nothing and admit nothing, except what everybody knows, that actual war exists, and that, as a Christian people, we mean to carry it on according to the usages of civilized nations.

The existing embarrassment is easily overcome. All further prosecutions can be stopped, and in respect to the privateersmen who have been convicted, the President, acting upon the suggestion of the Court that tried them, can, by the exercise of the pardoning power, relieve them from their position as criminals, and place them in that of prisoners of war.

In conclusion, we are not to forget that we are carrying on this war for the restoration of the Union, and that every act of aggression not essential to military success, will but separate more widely the two sections from each other, and increase the difficulty of cementing us again in one nationality. We are to remember that the people of the South, whose infirmity it has been to have very extravagant ideas of their own superiority, and whose contempt of the people of the North has been in proportion to their want of information respecting them,—have been hurried into their present position by the professional politicians and large landed proprietors, to whom they have hitherto been accustomed to confide the management of their public affairs; that, though prone to commit outrageous acts when under the influence of excitement, they are upon the whole a kindly and affectionate people, and have, when not blinded by passion, a very keen perception of their own interests; that there are, throughout the South, thousands of loyal hearts paralysed by the excitement around them, who still cling to the flag of their fathers and await the delivering stroke of our armies. Relying on our superior naval and military strength, and the settled determination of our people that this nation shall not be dismembered, we may, as the Swiss Cantons recently did in a similar crisis, put down this rebellion. That great duty imposes upon us all the exigencies of war, and they are greater and heavier than those which the Swiss Government had to contend with. We have to carry on the war against a people who have a large and well-appointed army, under skilful generals, acting on the defensive, in a country abounding with strategic points of defence. War, when conducted in accordance with the strictest usages of humanity, is, as all who have shared in the recent battles know, a sufficiently bloody business; and if we are to add to its horrors by hanging up all who fall into our hands as traitors or pirates, we leave the South no alternative but resistance to the last extremity; and should we ultimately triumph, we would have entailed upon us, as the consequences of such a policy, the bitter inheritance of maintaining a Government by force, over a people conquered, but not subdued.

Very truly yours,

CHARLES P. DALY.

www.ingramcontent.com/pod-product-compliance
Lightning Source LLC
LaVergne TN
LVHW020636110826
845149LV00004B/1233

*9781418190712*